Fathers and Sons

Edited by Liza Donnelly
and Michael Maslin

Ballantine Books New York

Introduction and compilation
Copyright © 1994 by Liza Donnelly and Michael Maslin

Grateful acknowledgment is made to *The New Yorker* for permission to reprint cartoons which, as indicated throughout this book, originally appeared in that magazine.

Some of the cartoons in this collection have appeared in the following periodicals and are reprinted by permission of the authors: *Harpers, OBG Management,* and *National Lampoon.*

Drawings by Art Spiegelman originally appeared in *Maus 1* © 1986 by Art Spiegelman. Published by Pantheon Books.

All rights reserved under International and Pan-American Copyright Conventions. Published in the United States by Ballantine Books, a division of Random House, Inc., New York, and simultaneously in Canada by Random House of Canada Limited, Toronto.

Library of Congress Catalog Card Number: 94-94046

ISBN: 0-345-38676-0

Cover illustration by Michael Maslin

Manufactured in the United States of America

First Edition: June 1994

10 9 8 7 6 5 4 3 2 1

INTRODUCTION

Fathers and sons are bonded for life by crazy glue. The father, himself forever a son, is shadowed by his father, and the son, whether or not he becomes a father, follows in his father's footsteps—at least for a while. The father–son team is a mystery, even to the team. Who better to explore the mystery than a crazy-quilt of cartoonists?

All thirty-six of the cartoonists gathered in this collection have experience as sons, and many of them have been tested as fathers. Whether they are exploring childhood or investigating parenthood, they're all, in their unique way, imparting pearls of wisdom, and—no small feat—making us laugh.

Our thanks for help in putting this collection together go to our editor at Ballantine, Joe Blades, and to Anne Hall, Christopher Shay, and Jill Frisch of *The New Yorker*, home to so many of the cartoonists who appear in this book. And finally, our thanks to the cartoonists themselves, without whom the following pages would merely be blank pieces of paper.

—Liza Donnelly and Michael Maslin

"Tom's really enjoying being a father."

Sidney Harris

"He'd be safer in daycare."

Danny Shanahan

"*I brought you up here today, son, because I wanted you to get a feel for the scope of this damned thing.*"

S. GROSS

Sam Gross

"I like things in the wrong place."

"It's now eight o'clock eastern quality time."

"*That's Evan, our youngest—he's just like his father.*"

"*Someday, my son, that will mean you.*"

"Wow, Dad, it's a beaut."

"I'm a little concerned—he's worked up a brochure on himself."

ANCHORDAD

Mick Stevens

"*Do that thing that you do, Billy, but this time do it the way I taught you.*"

Jack Ziegler

"Someday, Bobby, one-sixth of all of this will be yours."

"Now listen to your dad! If the sign says 'walk',
you walk. If the sign says 'don't walk', you don't
walk."

Bernard Schoenbaum

"*You want to grow up to be big and tall just like your dad, don't you, son?*"

Jack Ziegler

"Being a daddy isn't easy, I just make it look easy."

"Please, Daddy. I don't want to learn to use a computer."

"And that's how your mother and I met and fell in love. Your mother will now paint an entirely different picture."

Michael Maslin

"By the time you're seventeen we should have enough money to send you to college. Now all we have to do is figure out how to feed you till then."

"There are five elements, son—earth, air, fire, water, and women."

P.C. Mueller

"You call that hung by the chimney with care?"

"So, how are you enjoying your boyhood?"

"Okay, you can stay—but you're not to tell your mother what we do on hunting trips."

"Stop calling me 'Daddy Deer'!"

"Brad? This is your congressman. Get Mommy on the phone, please."

"Gee whizz, Dad! You hugged me this morning."

"We ought to spend more time together."

John Jonik

"Here comes the enigma."

"I'm afraid your mother has to work late again tonight. We do however have this video tape of her eating dinner with us last week!"

P.C. Vey

John Jonik

"Soon you will be entering a phase, son, in which you will no longer pay attention to anything I have to say. Please let me know when that changeover occurs."

"Please, Pop, can we go home?"

Edward Frascino

"Be a good little boy and tell Mommy where you buried Daddy!"

"*All right, I accidentally called you 'Rover'. Don't I sometimes call the dog 'Kevin'?*"

"*Know what I'm gonna do? I'm gonna pass my dream on to you.*"

Mick Stevens

"Miss Marspen, my son gave me a paperweight for my birthday. Could you drop everything and bring me a piece of paper?"

Tim Haggerty

"*I said 'no', young man, and when I say 'no',
sometimes I mean it.*"

Michael Maslin

"*I have to go to my grandfather's to show him how to use his new computer.*"

Boris Drucker

"What arrow?"

Jack Ziegler

P.C. VEY

"He's a great kid—and we have seventeen
thousand just like him at home."

"Son, I'd like to speak to you in my capacity as a father."

"My dad says I shouldn't take all that stuff I'm learning in kindergarten too seriously."

Donald Reilly

"Go ahead, Son, make a wish, but keep within the realm of possibility."

"He's got the Graupensteiner curse!"

Peter Porges

"Be thankful you're a bee, son, because it's all slugs and aphids down there."

"I was about to ask you the same question."

"My dad's a free-lance piper, but I intend to be a professional swine thief."

*"Here comes **daddy's** snorkel now!"*

Peter Porges

"It was a time when men regularly performed great feats of valor but were rarely in touch with their feelings."

"Son, you're all grown up now. You owe me two hundred and fourteen thousand dollars."

1

2

3

4

5

Edward Frascino

"Dear Timmy: Today the Dow Jones Industrial Average hit an all-time high. Trading was active on a volume of a hundred and seventy-five million shares, and the broader market indexes also rose. It was fun. Love, Daddy."

"*I'm sure you don't recognize my son.*"

"I appreciate your concern, Dad, but my commitment is to live with nature not to conquer it."

Henry Martin

Sidney Harris

"Two blood-rare sirloins and a bowl of rabbit food for Gautama Buddha here."

William Hamilton

"Look, son, real estate."

"*One of you boys go help Mom with the groceries.*"

*"Well, if you don't know the meaning of life, Dad,
then gosh, who does?"*

"The reason I don't hate my father is he hated his father!"

"Hi, Dad. Investment banking wasn't that great
after all."

Art Spiegelman

" 'A voice crying in the wilderness' would like to speak to you. I believe it's your son."

"Remember, son, it's not what you know that counts, but who I know."

Robert Mankoff

"Like my father, and my father's father, I know a great buy on slacks when I see one."

"I'm afraid, Son, this will never be yours. I'm having myself cloned."

"Young people frequently feel elated, son. This is perfectly healthy as long as they keep in mind that there isn't any valid reason for it."

BILTON & SON & GRANDSON & GREAT GRANDSON, INC.

"This was your great-grandfather's desk and this *was your great-grandfather."*

"Dad, do you mind if I call you Pop?"

"It's my son. He keeps me humble."

"C'mon, Dad—no fair! You promised I could name our next plaza."

Donald Reilly

*"Big date tonight, Dad. Can I borrow the
cardigan?"*

"I've been waiting a long time for that hug, Dad."

MICHAEL MASLIN and LIZA DONNELLY are perhaps the only married pair of cartoonists in the country. They met *because* of cartooning. Michael Maslin has been a regular contributor to *The New Yorker* since 1978. Liza Donnelly has also been a contributor to *The New Yorker* and many other publications. For Ballantine she compiled and edited *Mothers and Daughters*, showcasing America's foremost female cartoonists on that subject. Michael and Liza have teamed again to produce a new cartoon book for Ballantine: *Husbands and Wives*—coming early in 1995.